D0561330

# WET LEGS!

**Written by Nora Gaydos**
**Illustrated by BB Sams**

innovativeKids®

A hen.

A pet hen.

A red pet hen.

A red pet hen gets wet.

A red pet hen
begs and begs.

A red pet hen
begs to get in bed.

A red pet hen steps in bed.

WET LEGS!

No red pet hen in bed.

A red pet hen is in the pen.

# After You Read

Answer these questions about the story, and then use words from the story in fun, new ways!

1. What is the hen begging for?
   Why does the hen end up in the pen?

2. What other words rhyme with *hen*?
   What other words rhyme with *bed*?
   What other words rhyme with *wet*?

3. Make up a different sentence of your very own for each of these words: *red, beg, pen*.
   Now try to use all of those words together in *one* sentence!

# Skills in This Story

Vowel sound: short *e*
Sight words: *a, and, to, in, no, is, the*
Word ending: *-s*
Initial consonant blend: *st*

# ELK YELPS!

**Written by Nora Gaydos**
**Illustrated by BB Sams**

The elk.

The elk fell.

The elk fell on a sled.

The elk fell on a sled
next to a deck.

YELP, YELP!

The sled sped.

The elk on the sled
sped off the deck.

The sled gets a dent.

The elk is a mess.

The elk yells for help!

# After You Read

Answer these questions about the story, and then use words from the story in fun, new ways!

1.  What does the elk fall on?
    Why does the elk yell for help?

2.  What other words rhyme with *sled*?
    What other words rhyme with *deck*?
    What other words rhyme with *fell*?

3.  Make up a different sentence of your very own for each of these words: *elk, mess, help*.
    Now try to use all of those words together in *one* sentence!

# Skills in This Story

Vowel sound: short *e*
Sight words: *the, on, a, to, off, is, for*
Word ending: *-s*
Initial consonant blends: *sl, sp*
Final consonant blends: *-lk, -xt, -nt, -lp*